THE ASSASSINS

THE ASSASSINS

POEMS BY

FREDERIC PROKOSCH

AUTHOR OF

"THE ASIATICS"

Harper & Brothers Publishers

New York and London

1 9 3 6

THE ASSASSINS

Y

FIRST EDITION

TABLE OF CONTENTS

[v]

¶The author wishes to thank the editors of the following periodicals, in which certain of these poems appeared, for permitting them to be reprinted: *The Adelphi, The American Mercury, The Criterion, Harper's Magazine, The London Mercury, The New Republic, New Verse, Poetry, Programme* (Oriel College, Oxford), *The Spectator*.

THE ASSASSINS

THE ASSASSINS

O SUMMON out of memory
Into understanding
So that all may fear it
From the blood and fever
Of our passsionate and forever
Unregenerate spirit
Such spectacles
As men remember
Of the beautiful, musical
Of flesh, long, limber:
And deduce: how
In the consummate brow
Such cruelties dwell
As into eternity
Flushed the subservient blood,
Flattened our silver cities
And covered them with wood.

Consider, O lover,
The vistas you will find
Exploring through the years
Past precipice and river
The wilderness of the mind.
Quail! at the image

[1]

Of terrestrial beauty
More exalted than the eagle,
Than the lion more regal,
And contemplate
The planetary distress
That allows to move
Beneath such loveliness
Such hostility to love,
Such horror and hate:
O love

Remember Alexander,
Alcibiades,
Achilles: more slender
Than the slenderest of these,
Yet lovelier, still more haunting
Of voice, feature and form,
Vigilant and proud
As filled the memories
Of her who wildly stood
And discerned the centuries
Of warm ocean flood
So indifferently pouring
Past her constant and solitary
Egyptian shore:

And be reminded, in the hours
Of tenderness before sleep

By each beautiful stranger
Whether of word or flesh
How heaven has sheathed
By such creations our powers
In incalculably deep
And everlasting danger.

THE VOYAGE

GO SOUTH, they said, beyond the torrential islands,
And there at last you may find the concerted will
And the quiet heart, and the sure and sharpened spirit ...
And we roamed for years among the remotest places
     and we saw the still

Long misery of the maimed in the crumbling towers
And the prolonged weeping of women at water's edge
And the mourning in the desolate salt-marshes
And the trembling in the secret water caverns
     and the sighs in the sedge,

Heard the whimpering of the steers in the yellow valleys
And the grinding of teeth at noon on the spotted sand
And knew the sobbing at night in the blackened gorges
And the nightly squatting on slope beside the cactus
     and the withering hand,

Felt the wild-eyed longing among the enormous sea-birds
And the silvery listening to rhythm of ocean rise
And the shattering under the cliffs that shadow the ruins
And the ague of the whitened flesh in the starlit hours
     and the whitening eyes:

[4]

And the land grew white, white was the edge of ocean
And beyond the ocean silence rose like a reef.
Many the miles we had wandered, wonder at nightfall
Knowing, knitting our hands in terror, trembling
                    with love; with grief;

And finally, having come to the world's long boundary,
We waited, but saw nothing; waited, but no
Sound broke the huge stillness; and slowly turning
Saw only stars like snow on the endless prairie
                    and a sea of snow.

ALEXANDRIA

UNDER these leaves shadow
Spreads like a pool: cool
As a white shell on shore
Breaks through the leaves once more
The swan's obedient voice
And you beside me reach
Finger through finger slowly,
Only the hesitant sign
Of where we may begin;
Leaning our elbows on
The sweet deliberate lawn,
This is a space between
Waiting and waiting again
Yet still is happiness
Capped by the expected kiss,
The lunatic cramp, the novel
Hold and the white withdrawal:
Now in our anæsthetic
Calm, happy at sun
Warm upon watery breast,
Lulled to the water's music,
Limber with the siesta
Our reptile minds run on,

Dream of a time to come
When little's left to explore,
Love still remembered on earth,
The hairless stranger from
The agitated shore
Enters the central wood,
Feels Africa in his blood,
Stands stricken in horror
Seeing from nightmare stillness
In silvery confusion
Cataracts on and on
Slide like a caravan
And poised above his head
In leaves that dark gorilla
Waiting to clutch the traveller,
Hug him to earth and know
What through that heart does flow,
What compass point designs
Those glacial enervate lines,
What silver finger weighs
Such frozen silences.

DAYBREAK

LONG long ago, before our northern whales
   Grew dangerous when they glimpsed those slender boats
   Creep through the nightly waves,

All over Africa they lay awake,
The panther-eyed tribes, and feared the increasing twilight
Hours, suspecting magical

Modes to destroy, saw in each foreign whisper
Signs of a vast invasion, shadows terribly
Trampling the perilous dusk

Yet in the morning rubbed their innocent eyes,
Grew warm with tenderness and wound
Black arms among black arms:

Men, patterns of moving dust, loving those familiar
Limbs learned to think lovely, curves so tenderly
Shaped to receive and give,

Closed their long eyes, their thighs cooled in the old
Tribal water and cooled their dreams in unending
Memory, endless years.

THE DOLLS

I FOUND them lying on the shore,
Sweet shapes, pearl-lipped and crescent-eyed:
Night after night their hands implore
Pathetic mercies at my side.

They reach into my secret night
With pale and terrifying arms
And offer in a dark delight
Their subtle suicidal charms,

Gently they sigh into my mind
Wild words half uttered, half unsaid,
And when I dream of death I find
Small tears of glass upon my bed.

They are the children of desire,
They live on fear, they are my deep
And buried thoughts with eyes of fire,
They are the furies of my sleep.

ANDROMEDA

LONELY the long watch and the water's
  Music on the enormous shores,
  Lonely the isles and eastern stars,
Vega, the Lyre, the Seven Sisters:
Under her hair, her ivory hands,
Silent the cold Aegean sands,
Out of the ocean come to rest
Pearls on her fire-reflecting breast.
Lowering her lids through night she sees
Towers, pavilions, balconies,
Cities whose tender millions move
Through the vast labyrinths of love,
Each in his own peculiar pain
Lost on the hot inhabited plain;
Weeping with horror now she hears
Wings on the slowly silvering airs,
Gentlier than any mortal power
Ending the terrifying hour,
Suddenly warm the arriving day
Washing the wounds of night away.

EMPTY PROVINCES

WE SCALED the sacred hills in seventy days,
Carried the wounded with us and at last
Reached the dark land, the province of the lost,
Demanded shelter but their eastern eyes
Stared gently past us and their hands were silent:
One rose from slumber, turned his desolate head
And spoke, choosing his words with wonderful sadness
But what he said was hard to comprehend,
His lips were cracked with suffering; one approached us
Strong-limbed and graceful but he could not speak,
One held a shawl, one sang, one led his horses
Over the difficult earth with loving eyes
And one cried out in terrible tones how this
The Age of Passion now had killed the spirit,
One crossed a bridge and did a secret sign,
Grew suddenly calm, one crouched beside a fire
And wept with joy at memories of his children,
One smiled to see the beauty of a landscape,
One loved the birds and wished to be alone,
One scaled his yellow fishes and grew happy,
One told long tales of disenchanted cities,
And there were some who wept at how the nations
Had fallen like whores and spread their false allures
In hideous postures, one cried out at twilight

How dark as iron in our age comes love
And none are safe; how cloaked in dreams comes love,
Sighs through the coiling leaves and glides destroying
Through rumoured houses, intricate pavilions,
And as we travelled, leaving the stone terraces,
North to the wood, a land of wolves and otters,
None met us but their words remained for hours,
"Love's the great man, his brow is like the sea,
Only the fortunate know his constant anger."

THE CLIFFS

Norway's a shadow: sullen the cliffs at midnight,
    Stagnant the streams. Stare out beyond those fisted
    Rocks; whose features stung by disease and hatred
Now rise from the mother sea, the moth-winged silence:
What calm, what certainty?
                              O, far, far and far
Rise the loved towers whose revolving hands
Twine on our sleeping hours. In autumn, in rain,
They glide along the square, those sensitive footsteps,
Each one in dream familiar as music, fading,
Forever rising and falling, dreading, desiring;
What comfort, quiet?
                         Slight as the turtle's music,
Crossing those still star-loving fields, now circling
The pinnacles, flooding the gates, compelling the walls,
Great cities crumble, ocean to ocean cries,
All falls; what constancy, what understanding,
Now that the fiery and familiar planets
Tonight once more lie amorous on our rivers,
Slope fearfully across our ancient torrents,
And sting the night beyond our ice-locked islands?

THE WATCHER

BLACK and still under the Siberian heaven
Lies the lake: rise the reeds: sleep the herons
(Wings aware of the coming flight past the high
Altai); and the sands still; and not quite so still
The slopes cut by the icier streams where shadow
Covers the tread of the wolf, the quick nocturnal
Drinker; in shadow the streams descend through the wood
Now lapped in the birch's arm, now sweet with cedar:

Sweet and cool the pools in the hill, and still
The sleeping dove beside the unloving deep.

I can see veins in the dark flesh of the world,
Warm and nervous, colour of dusk, violet.
I can hear the quick beat of the tremulous moment
As the land turns, as the night wheels on and hovers.
Through the weeds of China shine the strange yet familiar
Lines of a face: the gaze, the trembling wet
Turn of the lips, the lids long parched with surrender
Which the years turn pale, which the night, the pale night,
    covers.

I recall the sigh of the silently falling cities,
I can hear the deer, the delicate, at the well.

THE FUNERAL

HAVING departed at the Hour of Morning
From the big gate that shaded the epileptics
They rode out through the hills breeding the poppies
       sweet in the red lands:

Breathing was hard in those cold caverns; but soon
They came to the salty sands and stones by the sands
Bitten to statues, odour of cinnamon heavy,
       hinting of lovers.

Then the tall spires through dream of that holiest of all
Cities still through the dawnlight savouring the moon,
Pestilence high on the canyon, billowing there those
       black shrouds awaiting

And the great brown warriors tense by the torrent, tall
Plunging, water-haired, eager for battle; the old
Beating their temples, burning their members, desolate
       down by the orchids;

The stallions glittering with terror, the lizards gold
In the ivies, catching the sunlight's lingering waterfall,
The maidens stained with their sex now bringing the sherbets
       sacred to converts:

And children slain on the cliffs, the ancestral hall
Black with the scattered ceremonial ashes.
High on the walls stood the perverts, dreams on their eyelids
       gilded and tragic:

Vestibules green with the fountains, loud with the zithers,
Harlots pale by the fig trees, and those mighty
Columns defaced with symbols; tainted; (mighty
       rose He from dust!)

The white dwarf whispering "Fly" and then that fœtid
Odour of unguents ripe in the neighbouring hamlets,
Already solemn, solemn, voice of the prophet
       high from the balcony,

Dead hour approaching, oaths by the tributaries, women
Washing their thighs with wine; and far, far
Out in the pools white with the snow of the ranges
       the snow-white heron.

THE PIAZZA

LABYRINTH, lonely corridors of our spirit
   Who wind through winter and night: neither the white
   Death of the stagnant centuries, nor the enormous
European fevers may thread and solve your allures.
I gaze from the edge of vast America
Toward the three continents twined in a common terror
Whose creatures still implore their nocturnal heroes:
A phrase toward the infinite, there as here: no more.

No more, it is all the same, all: nothing
Distinguishes my passion from those innumerable
Shapes in pairs or trios or utter isolation
Covering the city, in parks or story upon story,
Crossing the midnight seas, locked in huge prisons,
In taverns, towers, trenches awaiting the fire,
In chambers marked by the secret signs of the Romans
Or veiled from the vigilant Chinese constellations:

In which I rejoice: O darling, my limbs are happy
With power and delight in the uniform ways of man.
These lips which I love to all are lovely, these golden
Regions which hold my eyes and palms like a magnet
Are cast by the epochs of desire into such fragrance;

[17]

This gesture, lit by the intricate stars of summer,
Was dear to millions in equally still and desperate
Twilight, hot with the murderer breath of love.

THE ADRIATIC

BUT how at evening, autumn like a bittern
Winging the water, dusk without a wind
Hot on my arms, and your arms in my own,
The lapping on the shore, murmur of beetles,
Your hair still as a plant beside the thin
Scythe of the waterfall and scarcely recalled
Your voice below my lips sweet with caresses,
So good, hardly of day at all; how love
Made us aware of those half-hidden sleepers,
Rumours of other tribes more profligate,
The sighing furies, malignant silence covering
The suspected quarters of our twilit city,
Men in the silver nightmare of their long
Lanterned survival, and their slumbering wives
Who out of sorrow dream an amorous world,
Shyly approaching feel a gentle hand,
And nightly weaving through our wooded counties
The million breaths that issue through the gathering
Murmur of batwings, murmur of black leaves;
Yes it was love that made us understand,
Say Here, Come closer, Now, and love the fever
Summoned through miles of night by those long ships
Pointing toward islands their eternal keels,
Keen for the currents, indifferent to our tears.

[19]

THE AZORES

FOR another year now the wind's web of a far land
  Calms me who lie between two great continents
  Full of a fond excitement, hearing across the water
      And yellow sand
      Below my window

Cries from the past, bird, storm, current, great ship,
Dear voice and thought in Africa of love in a month to come,
Dark head remembered, whispers in the dark, embraces
      Nightly in another land
      And dreamed of nightly:

For another year, how happy leaning once more
By the pavilion, listening to swan's voice, silvery cataract,
Tread over gravel, young voice calling, shutting of a lantern
      And opening of a door
      All still remembered!

Yes, but I dream, I dream; from the deep orchestrations of war
Still rises what innocent we adored. But then that noise like
    glass
Of the falling towers, the great fashionable continental cities
      Along the doomed shore
      Falling like glass,

The masked surrender, the loathsome degradation within the
    tent,
The false exhaustion, the solitary spasm, the harrowing delay
And all those sexual sorrows, dreads, dreams, dissolutions and
            The vile abandonment
            Beside the misty bay.

Nightly perish on sea our friends, our mightiest and proudest
Ones. But no lamentation in the cities. No longer grieve or
    pray
For the frozen spirit: for those once iron who now like glass
            Shatter nightly, and by day
            Perish beneath black sea:

For here too we shall wander, here too the anxious and old
Will pass on their way, here too, fingers peaked in a
Forgotten gesture of prayer, lips imploring, bewildered
            As dolls and cold
            We too shall wander

Outward, and below the sun still resembling the golden
Glow when on summit white flicker of war appears (and
    then
All's done and still) and falling where the music of the
    world's
            Purposeless ocean rolled
            Once loved by a tribe.

[21]

LETTER

I STAND on the rock and look toward you in Ireland
  Through the travelling air: feel frost, hear waves, see fire:
  They spoke behind me of a time of darkness
Muttering of signs and wonders, how the birds
Streamed southward out of Austria, their wild warnings
Shrieked at the Danube water, and in France
A white child whispering of its nightmare secrets
Asked what they meant, weeping; none knew, not one.

I have lain with you in the murmuring stream and watched
The birds weaving their lines through the warlike nations
Who every night lie whispering like lovers
Hot and alone, have halted my horse beside the
Silent stream and suddenly beheld two great
Loving hawks fall limp out of the heavens;
And now I long for you and count our tender
Stars, warm doves, caught in this dangerous channel.

PORT SAID

Do you feel, shivering, the touch of the world's knife?
Look, cross the city, listen to the metal street,
Cross the black bridge and behold the water-haired
    women
        Grieving on the pebbles below, beating
        Their spotted linen, beating
        Their loins, listen to these feet

Climbing sadly the shaded path that curves
Over the water; the travellers watching the sands
For omens of war; the spies sloe-eyed and shuddering
        Like harlots; the negroes singing
        Of trouble, and beside them standing
        Those with the long white hands

Not male not female shaping the sign of Hermes:
Below, the expecting gorge: above, their eyes
Like pearls in the shell-white faces, thinking "Can it
        Be hard to die, is death
        A gentle lover?" and the girls lying
        In twos, whispering lies.

Not pleasant; think of those other cities; the dead ones;
The priests in their stained robes passing the urns, and the
    silken

[23]

Virgins bearing the frozen nectarines,
       Those led to the sacrifice, the
      Sufferers, the girls with the curling
      Tresses and eyes like pearls,

Sick of a dead world, and in the river the oarsmen
Naked and hairless, crying to the shepherds, old
Old men and wise; the divers bleeding, the widows
       Burning, the counsellors warning,
      The poëts singing the golden
      Princes, and how they told

Of another age, an age of silver, and that knife
Severing the race, that age of ice like a sheet over
The terrified towers and windowed cliffs and over
       The flowerlike bodies deprived
      Of spirit, gently covering
      Their solitude like a lover.

CHORUS

Torrent roaring through darkness toward the ocean,
Estuary in night, weariness, wilderness, woe,
Now at the end,

Past the gnarled shadows, shapes of other years
We go, having achieved the purity of our souls
And then finally

Entering that area where white ice begins
Shivering with light not sunlight, ice
Shaped from those very tears

Dropped by our grieving now attain the only
Safety which is the safety of those barbarous
Spaces beyond our moon.

Never again that clutching moment of error
Beside the bed, the oath on the mound, the horrid
Biting of buried flesh,

No, nor that fit of terror in the forest
Or the shrill drop of the net by the lagoon
Nor yet that melting

[25]

Thought, the awaited touch healing all wish for dying,
The true and loving gaze which sends our long
Hours of grief away.

THE delta rising, the isthmus widening, the waters drying,
 The dead devouring, the fever settling, the sufferers
  sighing,
The loved unloving, the loved unlonging, the living dying
And passion ended:
      pale in the fog that circles the channels
First of the second and then of the first gorge, sad by the river
We lay, sought over the rippled dark the routes out of China,
Followed the planets, the bells, the hooves of the caravan over
The terrible copper swamps of the high Irrawaddy. And then
Again, down through the defiles: past the gilt turrets: again
Lost in the tangles: and at last, the last great cities: the great
Dead cities beside the lakes, secret with weeds, sacred: the great
Living cities along the land's end, ocean-angered;
        the dead now conquered
By roots, moss burning among the moonstones, Buddha the
  lover
Smiling serene through the leaves in the cavern; the living
  covered
With men like moths, immense in the alleys and eyelids red
Like lips sighing unseeing into the half-lit cellars:
          the dead
Slowly destroying, the strong departing, beyond all bearing
The will subsiding, the swift decaying, desire not daring,

The dear ones dying, the balance trembling, the brave des-
     pairing:

And the lost cities, deep in the dead dark, no thought, no
     memory
Of forest moving, the imponderable laws of the planets
     weaving
Unchained, no change only the endlessly changing:
                                        the living
Bleak with impermanence, misery of change, green-foamed
     gutters
Emptying past Pnom-Penh. Forsaken. Men with the
     fluttering
Of the white moths move through the ague of living, all like
The light moth-winging in the wet jungle; nothing more;
     nothing.

Dusk on his eyes, the long ferns staining his temples, My
     brothers
Said the Prince autumn-eyed out of the cavern: Listen: all
Will come to me, some by the shrill swift road of suffering;
     some
By the mountainous northern road of doing, in deep night;
     the others
(Praying; the saddest, some of the proudest and strongest) by
The long white road of exhaustion. And when he'd ended
     no bird's call
Was left, nothing was left, nothing, the nettles black as the dry

[28]

Sigh of his eyes, night on his eyelids saying
                              This is the final dreading
Of history ending, an end to living and terror spreading,
The dead destroying, the living dying, the dream fulfilling,
The long night falling and knowledge failing and memory
    fading.

THE MASKS

SOME sit by ferns and gaze across their valley
   Counting the swallows loving on the gravel
   Or walk along the rocky beach, recall
A night beside the effigy in the garden,
The desire, the scent, the fall;

Or touch with closet fingers odorous volumes,
Children forever, clogged with solitude
Doze in the greenhouse, tremble at a rose,
Dream of their mothers when the winter darkens,
The wind, the big wind, blows.

Yes, in their Austrian houses sit the poets
And suffer at the passing of their heroes
Or in the Greek café beyond the noise
Of cheat and blackmail watch the panther-bellied
Girls, and the pensive boys;

Or wild grammarians travelling by the railway
Swift to the yellow cities on the Caspian
Blush, tremble; or the sisters who alone
Shed tears and on the entry of the Countess
Like owls rise and are gone.

Even among the natives those from Italy
Scatter and read their pages of an ancient
Epic, a great one, and with sterile hips
Dance; or in Utah weep before a mirror
With sensitive opened lips

Or in the ivied chamber count their syllables,
Stir toward the casement, watch the athletes passing;
Analyse love, as delicate as frost,
Talk to their girls in scholarly whispers, curious
Shift their grey eyes, are lost.

Some grow adroit at turning wheels, big women
Patient and proud deep in the Russian ices;
Or dream of Shelley, wishing he were here;
Nieces of millionaires, the undesired ones,
Year after maddening year

Grow stronger, glimpse at last the longed-for quiet
And talk with artists under April willows,
Find refuge in a masquerade of mind,
A pose, a flight toward dusk, smile like albinos,
And grow remote, grow blind.

The bones melt and the spirit breaks, the opium
Crosses the eastern sea and brings relief; and
Europe grows slim and pale; and we who loved
Her histories walk the city, wait and wonder,
Watch and are moved.

THE ISTHMUS

Europe is black; this ocean which curls like feather
Of fire on foam breaking along the peninsula's arm
Points toward the invisible

Watchers; behind me on the continent those dark men
Stooping by lamps above their warm and aching women
Stare at the seven sister cities

Frightened at dawn. Before me glide the fishermen,
Past their long white-veined fingers hardly human loving
The currents swift and strong

And beyond, the three black islands and the thirteen
Rocks whom the mortals fear, upon whose enduring scars
Now settle the stains of storm

And still beyond, that region known to birds,
White with their wonder, each cold whirlpool gently beck-
    oning
To those bleak eyes through night

Cleansed altogether from our ways of feeling:
And beyond these, nothing, nothing except that pure white
Space where the day

Grows one with night, both night and day forgotten,
Man's anguish flowing away, all save that enormous
Thought that eludes even the mightiest.

AFTER MIDNIGHT

NIGHT crawls over the lands betwixt Atlantic
And that deep musical sea whom men call peaceful:
The lanterns, visible dreams of men through darkness,
Now strive against the intolerable chill,
Night's mountainous whispers:

Upon our fields the glowworms, and the meadows
Sloping to south where lie the impatient lovers
Desiring darkness for their sweet exploring,
And by the lakes the watchers on the shore
Sheltering the candles

And vaster flames above the unravished woods,
Men who bear torches over snow and women
Crouched over the numb, licking the frozen toes,
The frozen cheeks caressing, crying against the
Torch-bearing heavens:

But hush: follow these darker clouds and see
In utter spiritual blackness the assassins:
Enormous cities whose ten thousand lamps
Console no traveller's weary solitary
Light-loving eyelids.

Make iron your nerves: the suffering, the insane
Here plot their spidery and destructive fevers
And wicked lovers yield; there is no hope
Except for those who now in uniform slumber
Watched by the planets

Dream of their fathers: O vast lord, protect them,
Let them forever so continue, forever
Assuage their tender tragical sleeping gestures
Calmed by the wind from your five seas, those fire-
Silvered companions.

THE TRAGEDIANS

ENTER the unremembered city:
Command before your eyes, call forth
To horrified sight those whom even the keenest
Among you have forgotten: stare:

Like gluttonous orchids flowering forth, and flooded
With emerald light: monstrous, tender, exact:
The child whose hands, strangely equipped for love,
Turn like a leaf to terror; yes, and he
Whom life has treated gently, now grown pallid,
Shapeless as water, a kinsman of the plant;
He who in tears remembers everything,
A thousand grey chicaneries and sorrows
Dimmed, but by weakness, not by time;
He who has learned to shape his daily love
Thus: a slow ritual of tongue and tooth
Crusted with evil; and the one who dreams
Only in the presence of watchers, whose bleak mind
Spills into being postures beyond all dread,
Horribly expert; he who lives in ice,
Motionless, thoughtless, utterly alone;
And darker than all, the old, the old and terribly
Wizened, whose hands reflect their caverns of grief,
Who gaze all day into the arteried glass
Of their habitual hopes.

Frail and enormous, hovering over the streets,
Creatures of air, revolting dreams? Fragments
Of night perhaps attending our nightly illusions?
But no. The city stands.
The actors still perform their feverish gestures.
Gaze, traveller, but say to yourself, Now only
Can I see clearly: say, Never and never
Shall the thoughts without words, the words
Without anger, the eyes without tears, the gestures
Without coherence spring and bud and flourish
Like the gigantic spurious mistletoe,
Tangle our actual world in borrowed shadow
And sponge all brightness out of the glittering air.

THE GOTHIC DUSK

THE Gothic dusk extends her serpent shadow:
   Ruined the hamlets on the northern shore,
   Ruined the walls of the entrancing cities,
Ruined the walls of the unhappy craftsmen,
Ruined the walls against the sea;
The walls of the Sunday-adoring village have vanished,
The walls of the liberal saints and the holy three;

Loathed and alone the gardens of the merchants,
The lawns of the limp and academic old,
Black the long halls of the philosophers,
Lovers of history, darlings of tradition,
And the Platonic grove.
Gaunt lie the pillared pools, defiled the fountains:
Fruits of a subtle and individual love.

That is the boundary of the dark: but daylight
Rolls like a flood across the Alaskan coast:
White the Illyrian cliffs and the Pontic ridges,
Down from Montana pour the enormous rivers
Out of their granite night,
The young are chanting on the edge of Syria,
Slowly the swamps of Mexico grow bright:

And further southward still the sun's dominion:
The darkening bodies on the foam-white sand,
White on the sand the terraces and towers,
Sparkling like foam the sails upon the water
And the watery music across the bay:
And beyond, the excited whispers of the prophets,
The domes of the hopeful glittering into day.

Yet over the daylight lands the eagles are desperate,
The ground is trembling, the gradual clouds assume
Those shapes half-legendary half-remembered;
Quick is the voice of the cricket, vast the ascending
Voice of the ocean in the shell
Tells the observant north and its dreary forests
How the dreams of the young grew fatal, and how they fell:

And "Listen," whisper the Alps and whistle the Andes,
"Be strong; the revengeful past will rise like a storm,
Breathe on our dreams, ask the intolerable question,
Demand the end of our quaint perverted idols:
Be strong, be brave as you will,
The ghosts will arrive, the tempests will be indifferent,
The streets will flicker, the asylums will be still."

THE RUINS

How strange, in sweetness and security,
The sudden advent of the enemy. Dream
Your silvery Scottish dawns, chin poised on finger-tips,
Eyes sweeping across the ruins gentle and solitary:
The tender life of exhaustion: fog has caressed
The abbey; violet the osiers and the meditations
Of men not quite awake. But then, how strange
The coming of a new and imbecile terror
Unreckoned even in our most romantic visions,
Bursting the secret dungeons of our history
Guarded through seasons of prayer and quietude.

Gaze down toward Italy: but remember the English
Deep in their moist nocturnal island, yielding
Strange forms of longing and fear, in pastoral shadow
Loving their landscape's arms and blossoming hair.
They too will suffer. Even those delicate meadows
Will witness a new abrupt hysteria; war
Red on the fields, the moors, the muttering woodlands.

Still by the Ionian columns, deep in ivy
The studious heart: still the quick-pivoting ankles
And calm the eyes, transfixed by yew;
Dark the submerging eddies, and the unuttered
Longing of our mother sea.

THE BALTIC SHORE

LONG, long the hours on the edge of darkness,
  But brief our trembling remembrance. Night. Listen.
  Again, soft through the blue October curtains
Detect the fragrant and familiar tread:
The breath on the brow, the warning word at the gateway,
The stride of the slender and immoderate dead:

Empty and dark those spells of agitation,
The fruitless spasm, the glance, the tremor, the word,
The street now silent, silent the church at midnight,
The clock's hand pointing, doomed the eyes in the square
Kissed once too often, the nightly rehearsed caresses,
The delicate fingers enclosing the trembling air.

Yes, frail the memory but frightful the unremembered
Sessions endured by those clasped in desire:
Long, long the pause upon the brink of silence,
The stare at the extended arms on the tender bed,
Never to emerge again the voluptuous spirits
From the kiss of the past, the embrace of the passionate dead.

Gaze: on the seas below the dear adorers,
Those fondled once on field, by cliff or water,
The huge and desolate eyes of the self-deceivers:

They loved their land, they struggled and they fell!
Now in their comprehending terror swaying
On the immense and equalizing swell:

Yet sways the man-entangled sea; and pale
Beyond the harbour slide the men through darkness.
Know the cold waves, love the cold finger-breaking
Dog-watch, the swell, the swing, the crest, the call,
The whine of the sail, the turn at the wheel, the aching
Eyes fastened on forgetfulness, the fall.

O spires, O streams, O sorrows, O temptations,
Those quaint and charming islands of our childhood!
Sweet days of indecision! but approaching
Crawls the curved drumbeat of our governing fears:
Huge heaven now slants on our diverted eyelids,
Night breaks to northward, ends the inconstant years.

THE SACRED WOOD

EMERGE from darkness, love,
And behold, limp from your surfeits, with languishing eyes
Such splendour as human memory can arouse
Out of our aching past: no storms rage here,
This is the garden beyond all seas and hurricanes,
These are the paths of wisdom, groves of passionate
Retreat; these fountains, the august images
Conjured out of our natural midnight hopes,
Plans for a future life. O, do not touch
These roses: they will shatter, with heavenly music
Enter the air and water; they are our gods.
Lovely of utterance, with eyes of unconquerable grief and
Poised with the grace of the enchanted, behold
These spirits who have guided across the centuries
The fragile and touching monuments of our solitude,
Our fears, despairs, philosophies, in a life
Too mad and miraculous to bear.

What land is this? This land
Is the land you have dreamed of, darling.
Don't you remember those pale towers, those long
And serpent channels, those tall rocks, those valleys
Fringed with our fears, those silent foam-entangled
Islands? This is the empire of our dreams

Where thoughts are snow and life is memory:
Silvery land of the dead:

O, flee.
Quickly from your remembrance carve all visions,
All dreamed of kingdoms, of refuge after the dissolution,
Of tenderness following despair, of life after death!

All loveliness lies in the passing; yes, eternity herself
Swings over the moment of perfection: be strong,
Dismiss all terror, plunge into visible love
Your energies and powers, all night, all day.

THE CONSPIRATORS

AND if the dead, and the dead
    Of spirit now join, and in their horrifying ritual
    Proceed till at laſt with oriental grace
End their concluding dance with the candles guttering,
The cymbals sobbing, the wind harassing the curtains,
The chill from the flood embracing the golden ſtairway,
The scent devoured and the bowls blown clean of incense:

Ah then, farewell, sweet northern music;
No longer the flight of the mind across the continents,
The dazzling flight of our words across the tempeſtuous
Black, or the firelit recital of a diſtant battle.

No. All that we loved is loſt, if the intricate
Languor of recolleċted centuries
Descends in its terrible sweetness on our limbs.
No shot will echo; no fire; no agonizing
Cry will resound in the city's thickẽts: only,
The ivy falling gently across the bridges,
The larches piercing the roofs, the reclining ſteeples,
The cellars rich with the agony of the reptiles,
The contemplative worms, the viċtorious rodents,
And at laſt, the climax entrancingly serene,
The inconclusive note drowned on the ascendant:

[45]

Our lovely shapes in marble still shine through the greenery,
Our exquisite silver bones still glide with the glaciers
That split our familiar hills, still fall with the avalanche
And weaving their vast wing's thunder over the Indies
The birds, the birds, sob for the time of man.

PASTORAL

HEART, from the furious thunder
 Of the storm-fingered winter,
 The tempest ear and eye,
Emerge into the tender
Spring of our secret wonder,
Close your young eyes and under
Their trembling night espy
The morning sun arousing
Again the golden lambs,
So lovingly the sleeping
Swans still within their feather
Shudder with feathery dreams;
Hear through the elms the echoing
Call of the hunter rippling
Across the delighted clover,
The fox still wet with dew
Moves through the infant day,
The lightning of the silver
Sun-inundated river
Startles the sleeping dove
And tender green where hover
The fitful moths and forever
Wanders the sleeping lover
Toward his awakening love;

[47]

And later with her lazy
Whisper the noon releasing
The bees upon the amazing
Gauze of the trees, surprising
There with their nervous music
The melancholy gazer;
And dusk the dear deceiver
Then soothes his curious fever,
Guides the inconstant world
Eyes closed and elbows curled
Into her merciful cover.
Lie on the edge of England,
Gaze toward the frightening sea,
Follow the twilight's flow
Out through the ambiguous plain
And the sweet April rain
Casting his shadows over
Our still protecting moon;
And then the shivering silver
Leaps through the leaves again,
Crosses again the river
Eager and cool forever.

THE DICTATORS

FRIGHTFUL dominions, sceptres
Wielded in the most utter of isolations: who, who
With muscles of iron, a lion's power, can leap
Beyond this rising torrent of words, vile music
Strung to disguise the autumn of our epoch?

But then: after the insinuations of
Yellow on the stalks, grey on the terraces, yellow
On the expiring saplings, the awful hue
Of yellow on the subsiding blades and our desires:
Then the quick shadow, the purple inertia still
As death; and storm; wind, rain, the Emperor
Superb at the moment of decision; we fall,
Suffer one instant the agony of extinction
And then no longer ourselves surrender, flow
Forever into the calm of universal endurance,
The end of misery, the death of all magnificence
Which history has awarded to our simple souls:
Driving through black from star to chilling star,
Dissolution of truth; by knife, by fire, by dream.

[49]

ELEGY

LONG by familiar channels, man-made rivers,
  Have watched, young fingers in the rippling glass
  Trailing, have sighed in storm-moist bed at night
With thought of words half-understood, those cruelly
Whispered smiles, the flesh withdrawn, the promised
Moment abandoned; have flushed with joy
At other's happiness on the rustic bridge,
The innocent kiss above the stream, the cattle
So gently moving through the reeds, warm sunlight
Odour of cloves; have laughed when in the barn
(Out on the fields the harvesters stood poised
Legs spread, arms brown or golden by the orchard)
You touched my hair and spoke, the indecent darkness
One moment winging us like a bat who lay
In inexperienced postures, aching heart,
Panting so like our elders in the fragrance
Of troubling things taught by another at evenings
Before the journey home; have walked at night
On errands of longing far across the snow,
Moved by the flutter of birds, of snow, and by the
Greyhounds, moon watering their backs, their leaping
Swift like a stream through silver woods; have climbed
At night the hickory, seen the beloved shape
Stoop at the mirror full of self-caresses,

[50]

Was touched to tears, suddenly soft and alien;
Have walked past country towns and pausing glimpsed
Those silent faces gazing across the reeds,
Doomed ones they were, I knew it, fearfully trembled,
Not understanding; have listened to the travellers
From eastern cities tell of curious ills,
The moneyed vices, accomplished gestures, nights
Spent in a delicate ordered self-destruction,
Disguises, double-entendres, and those hands
Hideous with habit, faces like a stain,
No realness left yet lovely in their sorrow;
Have sworn the usual oaths, still by their secret
Sign overcome and moved to courage; and then
The gradual suspense, surrender, not alone
Grew faithless, crossing arms beside the ivied
Pillars of our big youth; have heard those monstrous
Sirens and drumbeats ordering men to war,
No power to say no, worth nothing at all
Once the dark path is entered, faces void with
The grief of waste, the poverty of the spirit,
No good, no honesty left; have waited long
To hear the answer and been silent with joy
When saw the forgotten honour of my human
Race hinted at once more, shyly, not often
Visible to our eyes; but still that true
Masculine power not yet destroyed, have swelled
With pride, with longing, with that quick unutterable
Fear lest those mad ones once again rise upward,

Sprung out of discord all those monuments, steel
Sharp in the dusk of our constellation, yes,
Coiled in that serpent sleep beneath the explosion,
Rise furious and the end demand, the people
So painfully loved at last now plunged by those
Incendiaries, hasteners through our night
In emptiness, impenetrable fog.

SONG

How but by terror and love
　　Burst the shell from our eyes,
　　Rise from the adoring bed,
Thread the black shore, hear far
Behind the Arabian sighs
Of the vast and alluring dead?

How but by fear, more enduring
Than fervour of thought or thighs,
Sweep through the instinct's deep
Languor, learn to abhor
The tender entrancing cries
Of our souls forever asleep?

O prolongation of terror, O love,
Warm agonies of awakening, move
Hours, years, infinities
Of wandering, pity me, O bring
The iron and devastation of
The actual earth, the external seas.

HAND SET IN FOUNDRY GARAMOND AT THE
GOLDEN HIND PRESS AT MADISON NEW JERSEY
PRINTED & BOUND BY THE HADDON CRAFTSMEN
HARPER & BROTHERS PUBLISHERS
NEW YORK AND LONDON